BEFORE USING...

 A therapist's guide is enclosed loose with this book and should be removed and consulted before use.

To prevent bleed-through, it is recommended that water-based, rather than spirit-based, markers or pens be used in this Workbook.

DRINKING AND DRUGS IN MY FAMILY

A Hunter House Growth and Recovery Workbook
by Wendy Deaton, M.A., M.F.C.C.
Series consultant: Kendall Johnson, Ph.D.
Illustrated by Cecilia Bowman

ISBN 0-89793-152-1

ORDERING INFORMATION

Additional copies of this and other Growth and Recovery Workbooks may be obtained from Hunter House. Bulk discounts are available for professional offices and recognized organizations.

All single workbooks: $9.95   10-pack: $70.00
Workbook Library Special
(one of each workbook—10 total): $75.00

T0160002

THE GROWTH AND RECOVERY WORKBOOKS (GROW) SERIES

A creative, child-friendly program designed for use with elementary-school children, filled with original exercises to foster healing, self-understanding, and optimal growth.

Workbooks for children ages 9–12 include:

No More Hurt—provides a safe place for children who have been physically or sexually abused to explore and share their feelings

Living with My Family—helps children traumatized by domestic violence and family fights to identify and express their fears

Someone I Love Died—for children who have lost a loved one and who are dealing with grief, loss, and helplessness

A Separation in My Family—for children whose parents are separating or have already separated or divorced

Drinking and Drugs in My Family—for children who have family members who engage in regular alcohol and substance abuse

I Am a Survivor—for children who have survived an accident or fire, or a natural disaster such as a flood, hurricane, or earthquake

I Saw It Happen—for children who have witnessed a traumatic event such as a shooting at school, a frightening accident, or other violence

Workbooks for children ages 6–10 include:

**My Own Thoughts and Feelings (for Girls);
My Own Thoughts and Feelings (for Boys)**—for exploring suspected trauma and early symptoms of depression, low self-esteem, family conflict, maladjustment, and nonspecific dysfunction

My Own Thoughts on Stopping the Hurt—for exploring suspected trauma and communicating with young children who may have suffered physical or sexual abuse

We welcome suggestions for new and needed workbooks

DISCLAIMER

This book is intended as a treatment tool for use in a therapeutic setting. It is not intended to be utilized for diagnostic or investigative purposes. It is not designed for and should not be recommended or suggested for use in any unsupervised or self-help or self-therapy setting, group, or situation whatsoever. Any professionals who use this book are exercising their own professional judgment and take full responsibility for doing so.

You are SPECIAL.

Write or draw your
name here in a
special way
that you like.

This is your book.
In it you can tell about
yourself and your family.

_____

_____

_____

_____

_____

_____

_____

_____

_____

_____

_____

_____

_____

Make a list of special things you like about yourself.

Draw a picture of how you feel today.

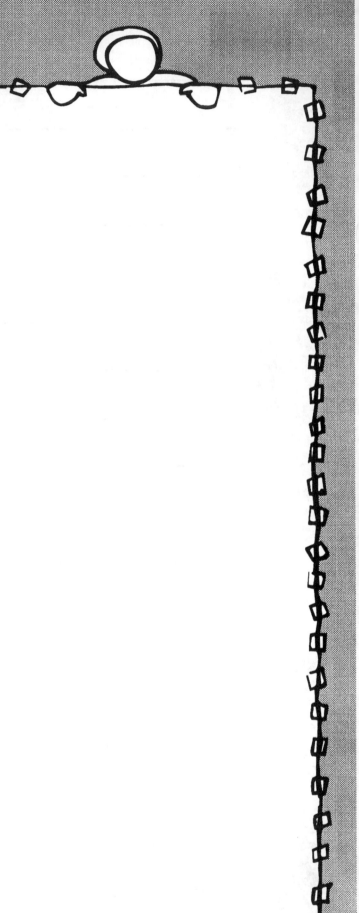

3

**Draw a picture of
your family.**

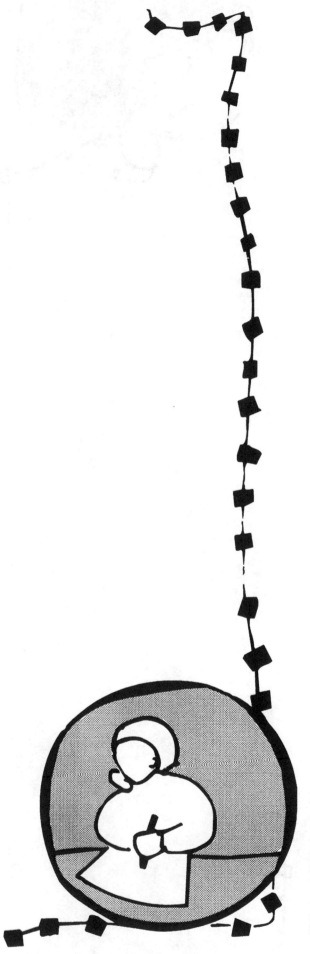

4

Draw a picture of your family
doing something together.

Every family has some kind of problems.
Here are problems a family may have:

- someone in the family died
- there is not enough money
- children are being hurt or abused
- parents are separated or divorced
- one of the children has a big problem
- someone in the family is very sick
- someone in the family drinks alcohol or uses drugs

Write others:

_____

_____

_____

_____

_____

_____

_____

Write or draw a picture
about a problem your
family has.

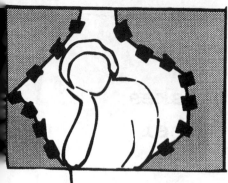

Write what you know about
drugs and alcohol.

_____

_____

_____

_____

_____

_____

_____

_____

_____

_____

_____

_____

A drug is something a person takes because they think they will feel better.

Many drugs are used to make your body feel better. These drugs are called medicines, and are like penicillin that you take for a cough or a cold.

Some people take other kinds of drugs just because they like the way the drug makes them feel— happy or sleepy or excited. These drugs are not medicines and they do not help anyone get over being sick.

Alcohol is a drug that people use because they like how it makes them feel. Marijuana and cocaine are two other drugs of this kind.

Drugs and alcohol are a problem when:

- somebody drinks too much or uses too many drugs

- somebody acts mean or angry when he or she is drinking or using drugs

- somebody falls asleep or "passes out" from drugs or alcohol

- someone is making himself or herself sick with drugs or alcohol

- someone is making other people unhappy or hurting other people by using drugs or alcohol

Other times:

_____

_____

_____

_____

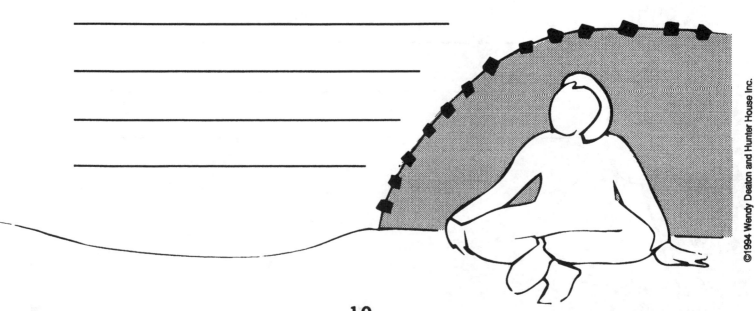

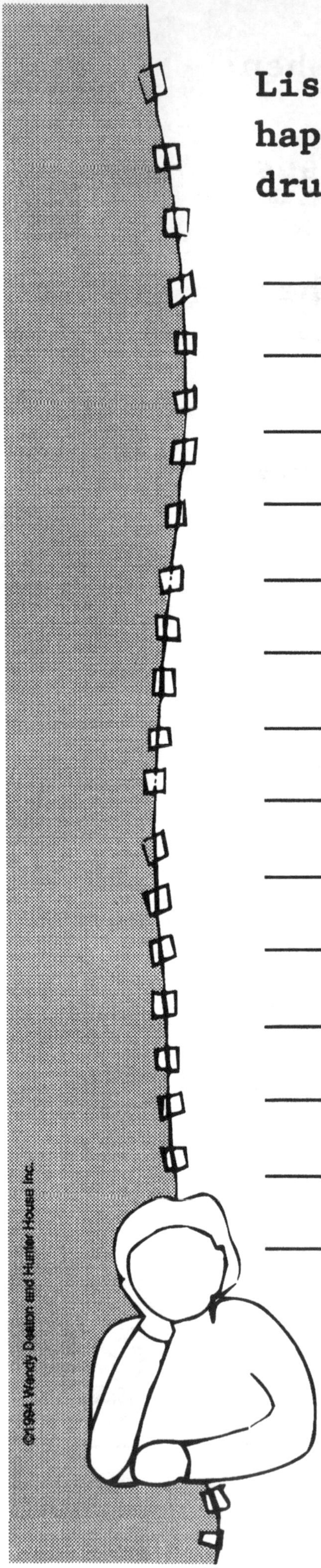

List all the problems that have happened in your family because of drugs or alcohol.

_____

_____

_____

_____

_____

_____

_____

_____

_____

_____

_____

_____

In the list below, check every person who is adding to the problem with drugs or alcohol in your family.

☐ mom

☐ dad   ☐ grandma or grandpa

☐ brother   ☐ uncle or aunt

☐ sister   ☐ dad's girlfriend

☐ me   ☐ mom's boyfriend

☐ other people:

_____

_____

_____

The names of persons who drink alcohol or use drugs are:

_____

_____

_____

Write what each person is doing to help cause the problem.

_____

_____

_____

_____

_____

_____

_____

_____

_____

_____

_____

Who have you talked to about the problem your family is having with drugs or alcohol?

_____

_____

_____

_____

_____

_____

_____

Write or draw a picture
to show how each person
acted when you told them
about the problem in
your family.

When someone you love drinks or uses drugs it makes you have a lot of mixed-up feelings. You might love the person but feel angry at them at the same time.

Check all the feelings you have had towards the person in your family who uses drugs or drinks alcohol:

- ▧ sad
- ▧ mad
- ▧ bad
- ▧ like yelling at them
- ▧ like crying
- ▧ like screaming
- ▧ loving
- ▧ confused

- ▧ scared
- ▧ helpless
- ▧ stupid
- ▧ lonely
- ▧ like helping
- ▧ like hitting
- ▧ hurt
- ▧ mean
- ▧ frustrated

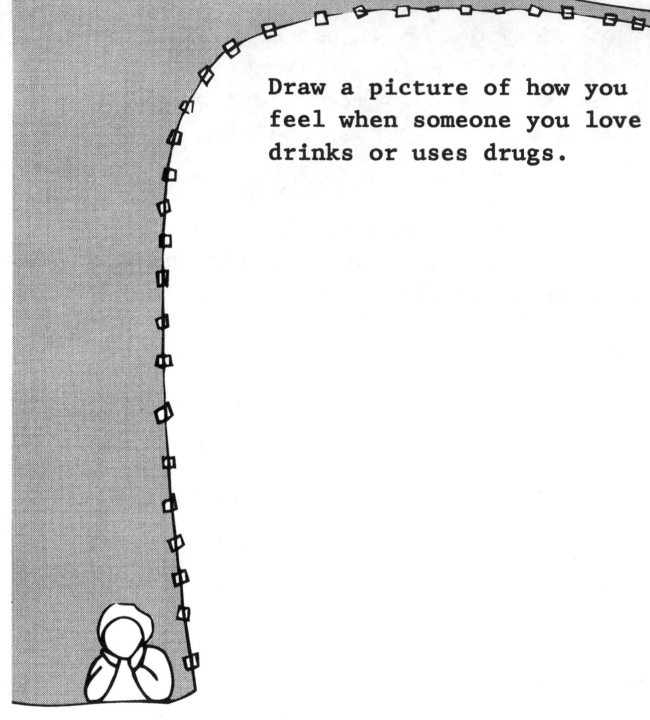

Draw a picture of how you feel when someone you love drinks or uses drugs.

When someone in the family drinks or uses drugs, it can make your life feel just like a roller coaster. Sometimes everything is wonderful, sometimes everything is terrible. Draw a picture of how your life feels here.

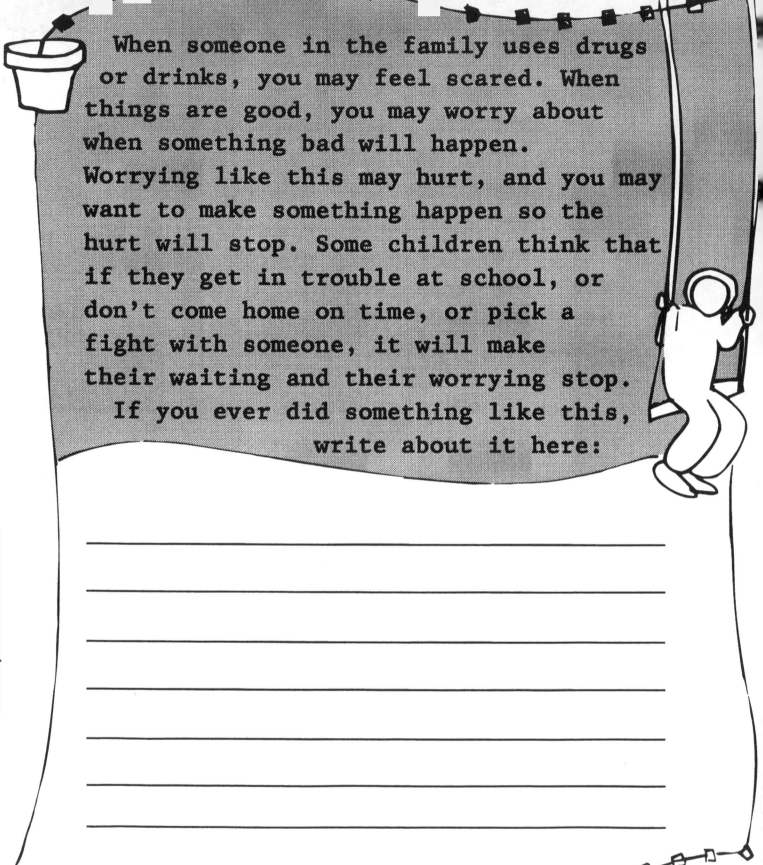

When someone in the family uses drugs or drinks, you may feel scared. When things are good, you may worry about when something bad will happen. Worrying like this may hurt, and you may want to make something happen so the hurt will stop. Some children think that if they get in trouble at school, or don't come home on time, or pick a fight with someone, it will make their waiting and their worrying stop.

If you ever did something like this, write about it here:

_____

_____

_____

_____

_____

_____

_____

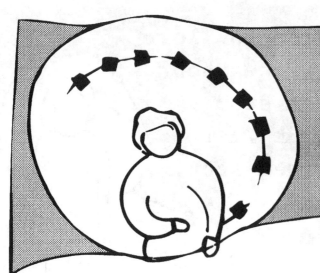

Have you ever thought you could make someone stop using drugs or alcohol?

Circle your answer and write about it.

yes   no   maybe

_____

_____

_____

_____

_____

_____

_____

_____

_____

_____

If you tried to make the person you love stop using drugs or alcohol write about it here. If you never tried to stop them but wanted to, write about what you want them to do to make them stop.

_____

_____

_____

_____

_____

_____

_____

_____

_____

_____

_____

_____

_____

_____

_____

_____

_____

_____

_____

_____

_____

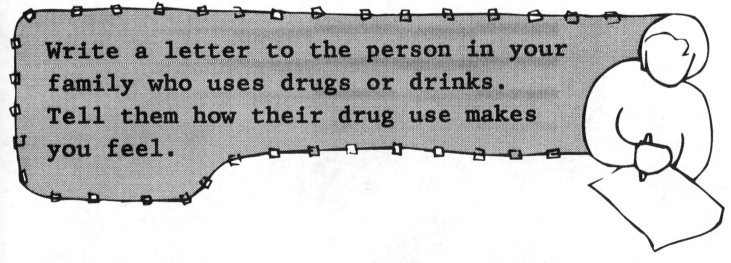

Write a letter to the person in your family who uses drugs or drinks. Tell them how their drug use makes you feel.

Draw a
picture for
the person to show
them how it makes you feel.

Here are some important things you can remember that can help you feel better:

- It is not your fault if someone you love uses drugs or drinks alcohol.

- It is not your fault if you cannot make them stop; stopping is their job, not yours.

- Your life might feel like a roller coaster sometimes but it is not your fault.

- It is okay if you don't want to tell everyone what is happening in your family, but you need someone you can talk to who can help you feel better.

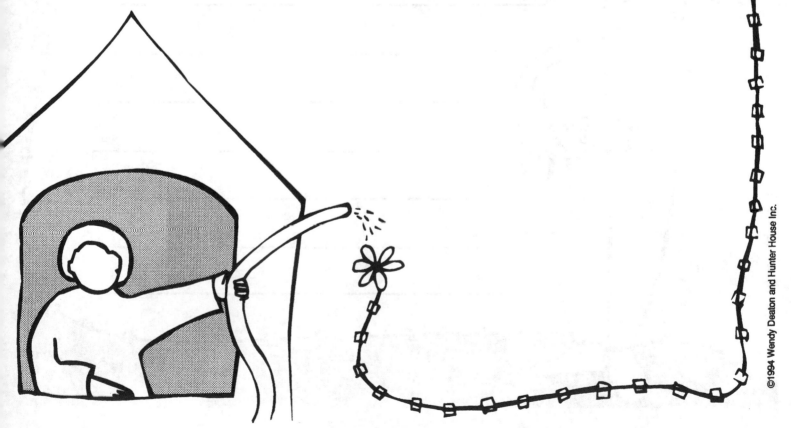

List anyone you know who can help you feel better about the drug and alcohol problem in your family. Write what they can do to help you.

_____

_____

_____

_____

_____

_____

_____

_____

_____

_____

_____

Maybe the person you love won't stop using drugs or drinking alcohol. Make a list of three things you can do that can make <u>you</u> feel better, even if the person doesn't stop:

Here are some ideas:

- join Alateen
- spend time with friends
- work hard and do well in school
- play sports or join a club
- go to church
- find a good friend to talk to
- keep a journal and write about your feelings when you are feeling sad or mad
- don't drink or use drugs

If you were in a race, what kind of a race would it be?

- ▢ running
- ▢ bicycle
- ▢ cars
- ▢ boats
- ▢ skateboards
- ▢ skis
- ▢ horses

others _____

_____

If you were in a game or sport, what would it be?

- ▢ soccer
- ▢ volleyball
- ▢ football
- ▢ softball
- ▢ basketball
- ▢ baseball
- ▢ tennis

others _____

_____

28

What are all the things you need to win?

- [ ] patience
- [ ] desire to win
- [ ] brains
- [ ] strength
- [ ] courage
- [ ] power
- [ ] practice

- [ ] luck
- [ ] bravery
- [ ] speed
- [ ] quick turns
- [ ] strong legs
- [ ] strong arms
- [ ] good eyes

Others

_____

_____

_____

These are some of the things that can help you with problems in your family and with any problems you have in the future.

Write a story about your family and give it a happy ending.

_____

_____

_____

_____

_____

_____

_____

_____

_____

_____

_____

Draw a picture of your favorite wish coming true.

31

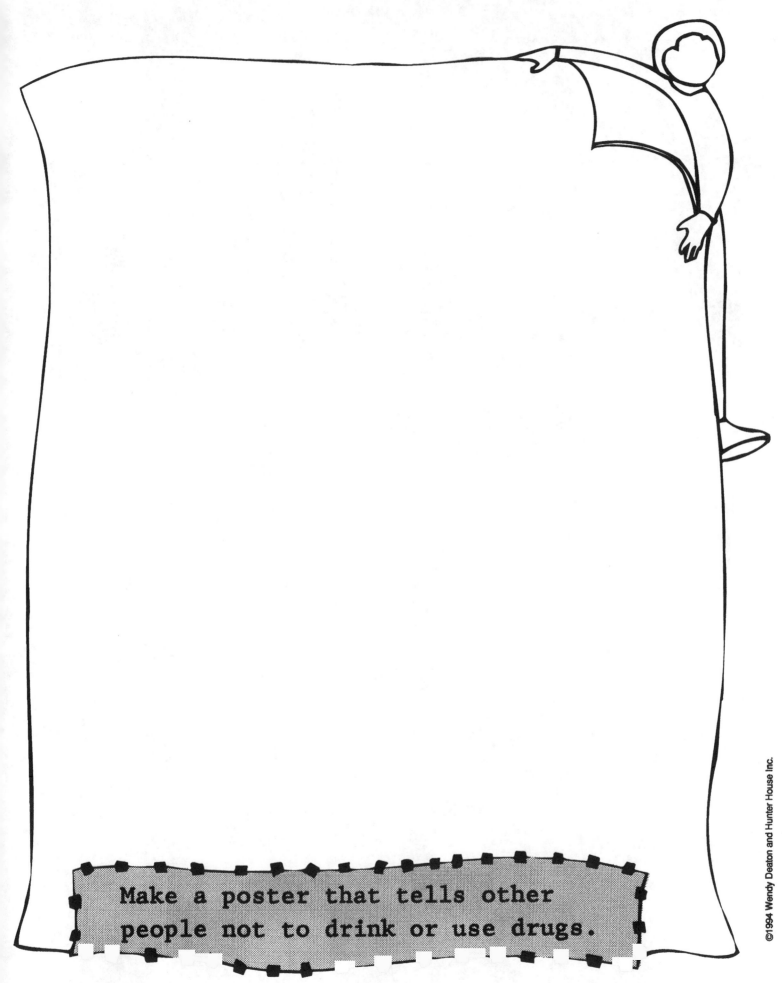

Make a poster that tells other people not to drink or use drugs.

Printed in the USA
CPSIA information can be obtained
at www.ICGtesting.com
JSHW051947231223
54110JS00023B/488